THE TRUTH I
TRIED TO
Outrun

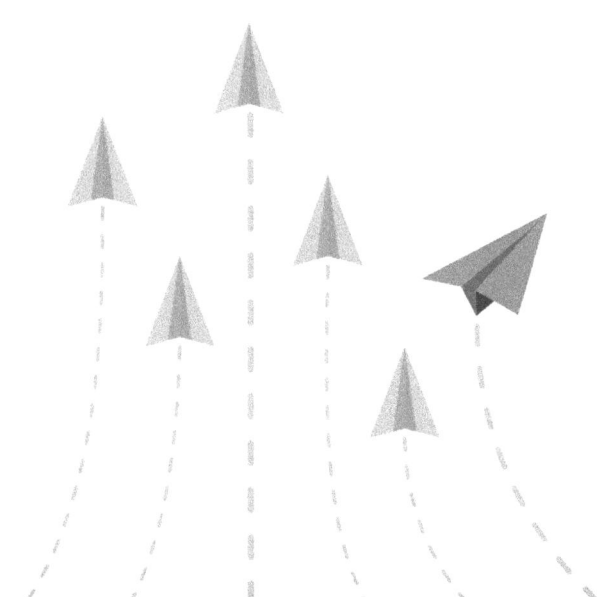

The Truth I Tried to Outrun: How Leaving Corporate Saved My Life

Copyright © 2025 Ronald Hale

Scripture has been used with reverence and care to honor the integrity and truth of God's Word.

ISBN: 979-8-9880626-9-1
LCCN: 2025921134

10 9 8 7 6 5 4 3 2 1

Printed in the United States of America
(Paperback) First Edition: November 2025

Author's Note

This book is a reflection of my own life, experiences, and personal perspective. The stories and thoughts shared here are true to the best of my memory, though memory itself can be imperfect. I have not used the names of individuals or organizations, and where connections might be drawn, they arise from my interpretation of events, not as definitive accounts.

Any resemblance to actual persons, living or deceased, or to specific events, is coincidental or a matter of personal perception. These pages are meant to express my journey, not to assign blame or make factual claims about others.

SITE PUBLISHING
7330 Staples Mill Road #106
Richmond, VA 23228

Author Information
Ronald Hale
Website: ronhalebooks.com
Email: sitepublishingtoday@gmail.com

Courage, faith, and purpose await you.

TABLE OF CONTENTS

INTRODUCTION

If you're holding this book, it's not by accident.

You were meant to find it: right here, right now.

This isn't a blueprint for building a house or designing a flawless life. It's a guide to something deeper: peace, clarity, and the kind of happiness your soul has craved for as long as you can remember.

This book may not be for everyone. But if you've ever looked successful on the outside while slowly falling apart on the inside — keep reading.

This is the story of how I got my peace back — and how I finally remembered who I was before the world told me who to be. How I tried to outrun the signs until they surrounded me, leaving me face-to-face with the truth I'd been avoiding.

Who am I? Probably someone just like you. I bought into the corporate dream: strive, work hard... but instead of joy, I found emptiness. After more than 20 years, I walked away from a six-figure job. On paper, I had everything I thought I wanted: a director title, work-from-home perks, and all the prestige that came with it. The corporate ladder stretched endlessly, and everyone assumed I should keep climbing. From the outside, it looked perfect. But inside, it was quietly eating me alive. Every day, I showed up with a smile that didn't reach my eyes, convincing myself I should be grateful, that I should feel fulfilled.

But the truth? I was drained: physically, emotionally, spiritually. The job that had once felt like a dream had turned into slow suffocation. I told myself it was just a season; that I could push through, that this is what "success" was supposed to feel like. And then I realized: I didn't have to keep living that way. *I had a choice. I could walk away.*

Then one afternoon, sitting alone in the cafeteria with my tray untouched, it hit me out of nowhere: I didn't even want this life anymore. Maybe I never really did. The noise of conversations around me felt distant, like I was in my own little bubble, facing a truth I couldn't ignore. And in that quiet space, I finally heard the voice inside me say, *"This isn't who you are."*

It rattled me. But it also freed me. For the first time, I realized I didn't have to prove anything to anyone. I was already enough.

My hope is that this book shines a light so bright that you can't hide from it. Not because it exposes you, but because it awakens you. You are called to greatness. Don't let fear, comfort, titles, or self-doubt stand in your way.

You didn't just find this book. It found you.

CHAPTER

One

THE DAY
I KNEW

I spent a little more than two decades climbing the corporate ladder: from traffic manager to print buyer, from coordinator to senior project manager, and finally, in March of 2022, I reached a major milestone: Director of Marketing. I was leading a team of nine, most of whom had been my peers just months earlier. It was a little awkward at first, having familiar faces now reporting to me, but I leaned into what I knew best: transparency, empathy, and presence. I didn't just want to be their boss. I wanted to be a leader they could trust.

And they did. Within a few short months, our team had built something special. There was respect, real collaboration, and a shared pride in what we were creating. We were producing beautiful, strategic marketing campaigns. We had flow. We had chemistry. We had fun.

But like any large company, organizational changes were inevitable. Between mid-2023 and late 2024, a span of just 15 months, there were five major changes. With each came layoffs or employees being shifted to other teams. Everyone felt the tension. Two questions hovered constantly: Will there be more changes? And should I be worried about my job?

We were given the same script to share with our teams:

> *Change is inevitable, but there's no news about our group.*

The truth? I knew just as little as they did. I worried about my own job too. Corporate America is cold like that: when the axe falls, you just hope it misses you. If it doesn't, well, that's your problem now.

With each restructure, I inherited new team members. And for the most part, we adapted and thrived. But leadership kept their cards close. We weren't in the know, but we kept pushing. It was always business as usual.

That momentum shifted hard in early 2025 when new leadership swept in. My manager, someone I deeply respected, was let go without warning. The team was shaken. The replacement was sharp and fast-moving, yet their style felt cold and abrupt. There was no warmth. No grace. It didn't take long to realize we were being watched. We weren't trusted.

Then came another shakeup: nearly all of my original team members were moved. Suddenly, I was leading a new group tied to a completely different part of the business. The people were brilliant, no doubt about it, but I was thrown into the deep end. There was minimal support and sky-high expectations. While other directors were offloading tasks, I was managing multiple, complex programs with the smallest team.

To make matters worse, four key players from the previous year's project weren't on my team anymore. Two had moved on. One was laid off. One quit. It felt like we were set up to fail. Still, I'm a praying man. I brought it all to God, trusting He would guide us through.

But the days got longer. The workload piled up. Resources were stretched thin. I raised concerns to leadership and was allowed to bring on a few contractors. But we were already sinking. And what no one understood was that we were stuck in quicksand from the last organizational change; no amount of extra hands could fix it now.

I've never been one to panic. Panic is contagious. But this was different. The choices being made at the top didn't reflect an understanding of the team's realities. It was no longer about the customers or the employees. It was all about the bottom line. The humanness was gone. It was time to sound the alarm. They had to know, and I knew I was the one who needed to tell them.

Despite my efforts, my concerns were dismissed. Three new contractors joined with little context, fast-paced on-boarding, and no time to catch up. It was like handing a newborn a fork and telling them to feed themselves. We were trying to steer the Titanic away from the iceberg, but we were too close. We all knew it.

Then came the unraveling.

A teammate of mine made a mistake. It was valid: another department raised the issue. I expected a one-on-one to sort it out. Instead, I was dropped into a high-level meeting with senior leaders. No warning. No prep. Just, "Join the call."

What followed felt like an ambush. I was grilled in front of executives. My leadership was questioned by my own manager. The one person who should've had my back. They didn't ask what happened. Responsibility was shifted onto my team member, and I was directed to report them to HR.

For me, it wasn't about finding solutions; it was about assigning blame.

Afterward, one of the participants on the call messaged me privately: "I'm sorry that happened to you."

I appreciated the empathy, even though they stayed silent in that meeting. Their quiet presence was a reminder that sometimes people care, but fear keeps them from stepping in. But the damage was done. I felt humiliated. Empty. After everything I had given — my time, ideas, nights, weekends, even my health — this was the response.

Still, I did what I'd always done. I regrouped and scheduled a meeting with my teammate, speaking honestly but without judgment. I said, *"I know this was a tough situation, and mistakes happen. What matters now is how we move forward… together."* I could hear the fear in their voice and the shame in their words—the same feelings I'd carried after being humiliated in that meeting. I listened as they explained what went wrong, asking questions to understand the situation, not to point fingers. Together, we mapped out a clear plan to fix the issue and prevent it from happening again. I made sure they knew they weren't alone—and that I still believed in them.

Until it happened again.

This time, it was a Teams message from my manager: *"Can we talk?"*

I joined the call. Camera on. There they were, with a colleague already on screen. No warning. No heads-up.

It was one of the most disrespectful conversations of my career. I was talked at; corrected in front of a peer, and treated like I didn't belong. My face burned — not from anger, but shame. It felt like a public scolding, dressed up as feedback.

I ended the call, closed my laptop, and sat in silence.

Then I called someone I trusted. Broke it all down.

"This has never happened to me before," I said. "Not once in all these years."

For the first time, I seriously considered quitting. I didn't have a backup plan.

But reality hit. My daughter was headed to college. Tuition was looming. Quitting felt reckless. I was a dad, a family man, I had responsibilities. So I stayed. A little longer.

Then came another emotionally draining meeting. More blame. More disrespect. I hit a wall. I was barely eating. By 5 p.m., I'd realize I'd only had a single bottle of water all day. I was disconnected. Worn out. Barely surviving.

I prayed. I called a close friend. I prayed again.

Eventually, I applied for 30 days of FMLA. I needed space to breathe, and time to visit my sick mother.

My manager reached out almost immediately. "Is everything okay?" they asked. We scheduled a meeting, and I told her the truth.

Then came the question: "Why are you using FMLA instead of PTO?"

I backpedaled. Said I'd cancel it. Told them I'd just take a week to visit my mom, who, at the time, was battling early-stage dementia, leukemia, kidney disease, and heart disease.

My heart was carrying more than anyone at work knew. And still, I kept showing up. For my team. For the deadlines. For everyone but me.

We had seven full-time staff, seven contractors, and massive deliverables on the line. Every time something slipped, the blame came back to me.

The way the organization had shifted, we were never set up to succeed. And I was tired of pretending otherwise.

During that week off, I made a decision. I listed the pros and cons of staying. And I started writing this book.

The cons list was twice as long. And far more damaging.

My peace, my health, my purpose — none of it could survive in that place anymore. I was shrinking to fit in. I didn't even recognize myself.

The thought of staying made me sick to my stomach.

That's when it hit me — I couldn't betray myself just to keep a title.

I couldn't trade my peace for a paycheck.

I loved that company. I gave it more than 20 years. But it was no longer the same. And neither was I.

They say people don't leave companies, they leave managers. In my case, that was true.

So, I made the hardest, and most liberating decision of my life.

I left.

Not because I had a plan. Not because I had it all figured out.

But because staying meant losing myself.

I didn't walk away from a six-figure job because I couldn't do it. I walked away because something inside me refused to stay a prisoner any longer. I had to convince the one person who still couldn't see beyond the visual — me.

This book is the story of how I got here. What it really means to walk away from safety, from status, from the life everyone else applauds, and choose yourself instead.

Because sometimes, the biggest risk isn't walking away. It's staying in something that's slowly destroying you.

CHAPTER
Two

THE CLIMB

I didn't stumble into corporate America. I earned my way in the old-fashioned way — through hard work, consistency, curiosity, and a deep belief in doing the right thing, even when no one was watching.

When I started at the company, I had no grand title or corner office. My early roles were hands-on, tactical, and behind the scenes: traffic manager, print buyer, marketing coordinator. I was the one handling the details no one saw but everyone depended on. There was no glamour, just grit. And I gave it everything I had.

What I didn't realize back then was that those early experiences were shaping the foundation of my leadership. Learning how to manage chaos, navigate difficult personalities, and solve problems quietly molded me into the kind of leader I had always needed. A fancy title doesn't make someone a leader. It just gives them a position. In over 20 years, I can count the truly great leaders I encountered on one hand.

Every project. Every deadline. Every team. I treated it like it mattered, because to me, it did. I wasn't chasing titles. I was chasing impact. And eventually, that kind of consistency opened doors. I moved into marketing manager roles, then senior project manager. My work was being noticed, not just because I delivered, but because I built relationships. People trusted me. Not because I was perfect, but because I was real and I got results.

Then came March 2022.

I was offered the role of Director of Marketing. It was the moment everything I had been building toward finally came together. I accepted the role with gratitude and a quiet fire in my belly: *Let's go. You got this.*

From day one, the challenge was clear: I was now leading a team that had recently been my peers. Nine direct reports. Nine relationships that needed to shift. I knew the optics could be tricky because not everyone celebrates your elevation when it comes from within. But I also knew who I was, and whose I was.

So I made a decision: I wouldn't try to prove anything. I'd just be me.

Transparent. Accessible. Present. I let them see the human behind the title. I asked questions. I listened. I celebrated their work and respected their boundaries. Slowly, trust began to build. And soon, we were firing on all cylinders.

We became a real team. There was laughter in meetings, pride in our work, and a deep sense of mutual respect. They knew I had their backs, and I knew they had mine.

It wasn't always easy. We managed high-pressure campaigns, impossible timelines, and constant pivots — the kind of work that burns teams out if there's no trust at the core. But somehow, we made it work. And we didn't just get the job done, we enjoyed doing it together. That, to me, was the epitome of success.

Looking back, I know this was one of the most fulfilling seasons of my entire career.

But even in the joy, I could feel something unsettling underneath. In corporate America, things can change fast. One shift in leadership can erase years of trust. One shift in power can tear down everything you've spent years building. And no matter how much heart you pour into your role, you can't protect yourself, or your team from the tides of change.

Still, before the chaos. Before the unraveling. I was thriving.

I had earned my seat at the table. And no one could say otherwise.

I didn't just climb the ladder. God made a way under every step I took. That's what made leaving so difficult. I wasn't walking away from a job I hated. I was walking away from one I had loved.

I didn't know it then, but every step of the climb; every late night, every challenge wasn't just about building a career. God was preparing me for something bigger. He was strengthening me for the moment I'd have to walk away, with my head held high, and trust Him completely.

CHAPTER
Three

BECOMING THE DIRECTOR

March 2022.

I still remember the call. The offer. The moment it all became real.

After nearly 18 years of pouring myself into the company, I had been promoted to Director of Marketing — a role that felt both earned and heavy. I had a deep sense of responsibility, but also a quiet confidence that God would be with me. I was ready to give this new team the same thing I had given the company for years — the best of me. I was also grateful to my manager for advocating for me. The title carried weight, yes, but it also came with a sense of validation. Someone saw the work. Someone saw *me*.

There wasn't much time to celebrate. I was now responsible for leading nine direct reports, most of whom had been my peers just weeks before. People I had sat next to in meetings, collaborated with on countless projects, and vented with during coffee breaks — now, they were looking to me for leadership.

That first week, I felt the tension. Not overt, and no one said anything out loud, but the question hung in the air: Can he lead us?

I didn't walk in like I had something to prove. I didn't pretend to have all the answers. Instead, I led with transparency. I told them what I was learning, where I needed their input, and what kind of leader I hoped to be, consistent, supportive, and real.

And I did something a lot of leaders forget to do — I listened.

I scheduled one-on-one meetings with each person and asked how they liked to work, what inspired them, what stressed them out. I wanted to understand their rhythms, their challenges, and their wins — not just as employees, but as people. My goal wasn't to micromanage them. It was to grow them. To pull out the very best in them as I gave my best.

And slowly, things began to shift. The tension eased. Conversations opened up. Feedback flowed in both directions. I was no longer the colleague-turned-boss. I was their leader. Not because of a title, but because I had earned their trust.

We found a rhythm that worked. One that wasn't conventional but was inspiring. For the first time in the new role, I felt like I was part of something bigger than myself.

I made it clear — I didn't have to be the smartest person in the room. They were the subject matter experts, and it was my job to make their jobs easier. We weren't just doing great work, we were thriving. Creativity sparked. Collaboration flowed. We had each other's backs.

Of course, there were hard days. Marketing always has pressure. But no one was carrying the weight alone. We solved problems together. We laughed in meetings. We celebrated small wins. We cared. We were family.

I remember one campaign in particular. The scope was massive, and the timelines were brutal. But everyone pulled together, stayed late, and delivered something we were genuinely proud of. I walked away from that project thinking: *This is it. This is what leadership is supposed to feel like.*

I had always believed in servant leadership, empowering, not micromanaging; building confidence, not barking orders. And it was working.

There's this myth in corporate America that when you reach a certain level, you have to become more distant, more polished, more "executive." But I chose a different path. I stayed human. I led with empathy. And my team responded with loyalty and excellence.

It wasn't just about KPIs and deadlines. It was about people. About culture. About trust.

In those early months, I truly believed I had found my sweet spot — a role that matched my passion, a team that reflected my values, and a future that felt full of promise. The sky was the limit and together we were reaching heights no one knew was possible.

I didn't realize we were standing in the calm before the storm. I had no idea how quickly things could change. How fast the air could be sucked out of a room. How the thing you once loved could become the very thing that drains you.

It started with one loss.

We had a team member who was a natural leader. A standout. I went to leadership again and again advocating for their promotion. But every time, I was told the same thing — "Give it time."

Month after month, I made the case. This person wasn't just good at their job, they made the whole team better. But I kept hitting a wall. The excuses didn't match the performance. Maybe it was because I was new in the role. Maybe they didn't trust me yet. But whatever the reason, my voice wasn't enough.

By the fourth rejection, something in me shifted. I realized the title of Director didn't hold the influence I thought it did. It looked good on paper, but in the moments that mattered, it meant nothing.

A month later, I got the call no manager wants. That same team member had accepted a job offer – a larger role, better pay, and worst of all, with a competitor.

They didn't want to leave. I knew that. But I couldn't give them what they needed. I tried to convince them to stay, but the damage was done. The opportunity was gone.

I called my manager right away.

"They're leaving," I said.

Their response? "Let them go."

I blinked. "What?"

"They've made their choice. Let them go."

I was stunned. This person was one of our best. Respected. Trusted. Talented. And yet, it didn't matter. Their value didn't move the needle where it counted. That moment taught me something I'll never forget — leading in corporate America is not for the faint of heart.

Still, I held onto those early days. That sense of pride. That momentum. Because it reminded me of who I was as a leader. Even after losing a key player, that would never change.

Leadership, to me, has never been about control. it's about creating an environment where others can shine. And for a while, that's exactly what we had.

I would've stayed for that version of the job forever.

But that version didn't last.

CHAPTER
Four

WHEN THE WINDS CHANGED

I've learned that in corporate America change doesn't always announce itself with a bang. Sometimes it comes in quietly tucked inside strategy decks and ushered in by confident new faces. By the time you realize what's happening, you're already knee-deep in something you didn't ask for.

That's how it started in early 2025.

One day, I had a manager I respected — someone who challenged me, supported me, and trusted my leadership — and then, just like that, they were gone. Laid off. No warning. No transition plan. Just a message that they were no longer with the company.

It was the first major crack in what had once felt like solid ground.

Soon after, we met our new leader. From our first interaction, I knew this would be different. Fast-moving. Sharp. Clearly someone who knew how to climb. But their communication? Cold. Direct. Often dismissive. They never asked what we needed, only what we had done, or failed to do. No effort to build rapport. No understanding of our team's culture. No acknowledgment of the groundwork we had already laid.

Suddenly, it felt like none of the work we'd done, none of the trust, none of the wins, really mattered anymore. For the first time in 20+ years, I felt like an outsider. Like my opinion didn't matter. Like I was no longer part of the team.

Still, I did what I'd always done: adapt. Keep moving. Make it work.

Then came the restructuring.

I was assigned an entirely new line of business. New team members. New expectations. New pressure. I still managed three members from my original group, but now also oversaw marketing initiatives for an entirely unfamiliar department.

I didn't flinch. I rolled up my sleeves, leaned into the learning curve, and committed to earning the new team's trust, just like I had before. And remarkably, I did.

I found myself surrounded again by smart, talented people who wanted to do great work. We were buried in high-stakes initiatives, overwhelmed at times, but moving forward, together.

The problem wasn't the team. It was the culture shifting above us.

Where there had once been collaboration, there was now silencing. Where there had been transparency, there was secrecy. Leadership meetings felt more like interrogations than discussions. Conversations were one-sided. Where feedback was once a tool, it had become a weapon.

The first real blow came during a cross-functional meeting. In hindsight, it felt like a setup. One of my team members had made a blatant mistake. The concern raised was valid, and I came prepared to address it with integrity. I expected a solution-oriented conversation.

Instead, I walked into an ambush — a Teams call full of senior leaders, ready to point fingers. My employee was being humiliated by something that could have been solved with a quick call. And the worst part? My own leader joined in. No support. No fairness. Just blame.

It felt like I was on a virtual firing squad, and I was the one in the crosshairs.

When I tried to speak up in defense of my employee, I was reprimanded. Dismissed. Sent to the "principal's office" for having an opinion. It was humiliating. It was infuriating. And in that moment, I knew — I needed an exit strategy from corporate America, for good.

I had never faced anything like this before. For over twenty years, my record was spotless. I was the one people trusted, the one who delivered results, the one leaders counted on. But that day, it didn't matter. I felt like a human dartboard, stuck in place while the darts kept coming. I couldn't move. I couldn't defend myself.

And it wasn't the criticism that hurt—I knew how to take feedback. This was different. This was about control, not care. Optics over truth. Power over people. It was a game I didn't want to play, but I had been forced onto the board.

Something inside me broke that day, and I knew it wouldn't go back to the way it was. The trust was gone—not with my team, but with the system above me. With my new leader. And when trust breaks, it changes how you see everything.

I started avoiding certain meetings, protecting my energy, staying out of the line of fire. I kept my head down, but in my heart, I knew the truth: no matter what we did, my team and I would always be presumed guilty before we were ever proven innocent.

Every meeting grew heavier. Every decision was more political. Every conversation felt like it might be used against you. It was a high-pressure, low-compassion environment — a deadly combination.

And no matter how hard I worked, or how much I accomplished, it became clear I was no longer being seen as a leader. I was being watched.

The winds had changed.

And though I hadn't yet admitted it out loud, even to myself, I knew something deep down — this wasn't the job I signed up for anymore.

In corporate America, they tell you to be flexible. To adapt. To embrace change.

But what they don't tell you is that some changes aren't worth adapting to.

Some change erodes the very foundation of why you're there in the first place.

And eventually, even the strongest leader has to ask — *At what cost? What is this worth to me?*

I didn't realize it at the time, but God was already preparing me to leave. The control, the silencing, the humiliation, it wasn't just hardship. It was Him revealing what I could no longer ignore. When the winds changed, I had a choice to make — stay loyal to a system that no longer honored who I was or follow the One who always had. It wasn't just about walking away from a job. It was about walking toward the truth.

CHAPTER
Five

A TEAM WORTH
FIGHTING FOR

When everything else threatened to break me, it was God, and the unshakable loyalty of my team that kept me standing.

Despite the dysfunction swirling above us, they still showed up, fully. With heart, creativity, and commitment. They kept producing strong work. They collaborated. They looked out for each other. Even as the culture shifted around us, *we stayed grounded*. For a while.

That loyalty wasn't an accident. It was built.

I had spent over a year cultivating something rare in corporate America — a team that felt like family. We checked in when someone went quiet. We celebrated birthdays and little wins. And when things went sideways, we didn't play the blame game. We owned it. We learned. We moved on together.

So, when everything else started to feel unstable, I didn't retreat, I protected. I doubled down. Not on projects, but on people.

Even as pressure mounted from above — even as impromptu meetings blindsided me — even as my credibility came under quiet attack, I tried to shield them. I kept the chaos from trickling down. They never saw the cost of caring deeply while being pulled apart — not because I was hiding, but because I didn't want them to feel it. That was my responsibility.

That's what leaders do, right?

But the truth is, I was drowning.

Emotionally, I was depleted. Spiritually, I was drained. Most days I worked through lunch, barely eating. I used to go through several bottles of water a day. Now? Maybe one. I felt myself shrinking, becoming more robotic, less present. Just making it through the day felt like a win.

And yet... I stayed.

Because of them.

Because I knew what they were juggling — massive projects, impossible timelines, cross-functional tension, and constant change. At that point, I was leading seven full-time employees and seven contractors. We weren't just producing content. We were powering campaigns. Driving company-wide initiatives. Holding things together during a time of total disruption.

But we were never recognized for it.

If anything went wrong, even outside our control, we were the first ones blamed. Or worse, I was. It didn't matter how many times we delivered. The default posture from above was still distrust.

There's a unique kind of pain in leading a high-performing team that's being quietly undermined. You start to wonder, *Is it me?* You try harder. You work longer hours. You absorb more than you should. And every time you get knocked down, you find a way to get back up, because they're watching you.

But what no one tells you about leading with heart… is how lonely it can feel when the system doesn't care.

I was becoming the buffer between chaos and calm, dysfunction and delivery, leadership and team. And it was slowly breaking me.

What I loved most about leadership was lifting others. But now, no one was lifting me, except my team.

Still, I stayed. Because I loved them. Because they loved the work. Because we were still building things we believed in. And because walking away felt like abandoning them in a place that was getting harder by the day.

That's what most people don't understand about leaving a role like mine. It's not just about the title or the paycheck. It's about the people. The ones who trusted you. The ones you protected. The ones who looked to you for leadership, support, and strength.

You don't leave a team like that without grieving it first.

So every time I thought about resigning, I'd picture their faces. And I'd tell myself, *Just one more week.*

But the cracks were getting wider. And no amount of passion could plaster over a broken system forever. I didn't know how much longer I could keep showing up for everyone else… when no one seemed to notice that I was barely holding it together.

Leadership *is* a privilege. I still believe that.

But leadership without support becomes a slow form of self-sacrifice. And eventually, I had to ask myself: At what point does loyalty to others become betrayal of self?

CHAPTER
Six

MEETINGS THAT WOUND

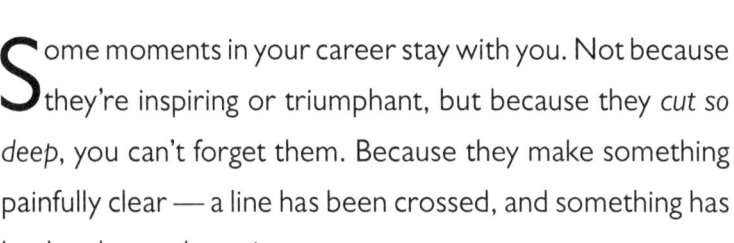

Some moments in your career stay with you. Not because they're inspiring or triumphant, but because they *cut so deep*, you can't forget them. Because they make something painfully clear — a line has been crossed, and something has broken beyond repair.

For me, one of those moments happened on a random Thursday. It started like any other. A simple Teams message from my manager, "Hey, can you jump on a call?"

No subject. No details. Nothing unusual. But something in my gut told me this wasn't just a check-in.

I joined the video meeting, turned on my camera, and immediately noticed another colleague on the call. One who had never been on a one-on-one between me and my manager before. The look on their face said more than words ever could.

My stomach dropped.

This wasn't business as usual. This was something else entirely. The only thought running through my mind was —

What now?

What followed wasn't just uncomfortable, it was humiliating. I was criticized harshly, questioned unfairly, and spoken to as if I were *incompetent* — not as a seasoned leader. Not as someone who had given nearly two decades of his life to the company. But as someone disposable. Someone who needed to be corrected.

And worse? It happened in front of a peer.

I wasn't just being reprimanded. I was being publicly dismantled. Not because of performance—but because of power. This wasn't feedback. This was control.

I don't remember every word, but I'll never forget how I felt — Small. Embarrassed. Undone.

When the call ended, I sat in silence. My face was flushed. My heart was pounding. I just stared at the screen, trying to process what had just happened. Then, I did something I almost never did during work hours, I called my best friend.

No "hello."

Just an exhale.

And then I said, "I think I'm done."

It was the first time I'd said those words out loud. Not because I couldn't handle pressure. I'd been handling pressure my whole life. And not because I didn't believe in myself. I did. But because it finally hit me — they didn't believe in me.

They questioned the one thing I held most sacred in my career — my integrity.

And just as devastating, they no longer respected me.

That meeting shook something loose in me. Things I had tolerated for too long. The tone, the micromanagement, the lack of grace, were no longer background noise. They were *personal*.

That wasn't just a meeting. That was a line being crossed.

Still, I tried to move forward. I told myself it was a bad day. A misstep. Maybe I could recover. Maybe *they could*, too.

But then came the second call.

Another unannounced meeting.

Another public teardown.

Another moment where I was blindsided and belittled.

No collaboration.

No clarity.

Just confrontation.

After that, I was emotionally drained. Not just by what happened, but by what didn't. There was no apology, no ownership, no acknowledgment that maybe, just maybe, the way I was being treated was wrong.

What hurt the most wasn't what was said. It was the disregard for my humanity.

I had worked too hard. Sacrificed too much. Shown up consistently, with care, with integrity, with excellence.

And now? I felt reduced to a line item on someone else's to-do list.

No context.

No grace.

No respect.

After that second meeting, I couldn't pretend anymore. The stress started showing up in my body — fatigue, headaches, tightness in my chest. I felt heavy all the time. Even at home.

I was no longer showing up to lead. I was showing up to survive. Meetings felt like landmines. Emails made my heart race. I was constantly bracing for the next blow.

This wasn't burnout.

This wasn't insecurity.

This was betrayal.

And for someone like me, someone who had always protected his people, always led with heart — that kind of breach doesn't just sting. It *wounds*.

I used to enter meetings ready to solve problems. Now, I entered them ready to *defend myself*.

And that's when I knew something had to give.

The most painful meetings aren't the ones where you get tough feedback. They're the ones where you realize you're no longer being seen.

And once you're invisible to the people who control your future, the only power you have left is choosing to walk away.

CHAPTER

Seven

BREAKING POINT

There's a moment in every storm when the calm shatters, and you realize you can't keep pretending everything's fine.

For me, that moment didn't come with thunder or a dramatic collapse. It came quietly, like a weight settling in my chest that wouldn't go away.

I had given this job more than twenty years of my life.

I climbed the ladder, earned the titles, and built teams I was proud of. On paper, it looked like success. But somewhere along the way, I started losing pieces of myself.

It wasn't just the toxic meetings, the micromanagement, or the subtle humiliations. It was the slow erosion of my peace, my purpose, and my joy.

I wasn't just tired. I was depleted — mentally, emotionally, and spiritually.

Each day felt like a battle, not with the work, but with the environment. The fear of losing my job, the pressure to perform, the constant scrutiny, it was suffocating.

And in the silence of my thoughts, the questions grew louder:

Who am I now?

What's left of me?

Is this the life I want to keep living?

The breaking point wasn't a dramatic exit. It was a series of quiet, sobering truths I could no longer ignore:

I wasn't thriving, I was just surviving.

I wasn't respected, I was barely tolerated.

I wasn't fulfilled, I was running on fumes.

I thought about my daughter: the future I wanted her to see and believe was possible.

I thought about my family and friends. The ones who reminded me of who I was when I couldn't remember.

And I thought about the man I used to be — the one who walked into rooms with confidence, who believed in hard work, who led with integrity.

Was he gone? Or was he still in there, waiting for me to find him again?

The answers didn't come in a flash. They came slowly, through honest conversations, sleepless nights, and still moments with God.

I realized that staying in this job, in this environment, was no longer an act of loyalty to myself. *It was an act of self-destruction.*

I wasn't leaving because I gave up. I was leaving because I woke up. Because I had the wisdom to choose wholeness over burnout, courage over comfort.

Because sometimes, the bravest thing you can do is walk away from something you once loved, when it no longer loves you back.

The decision wasn't easy. Fear and uncertainty pulled at me, and twenty years of memories refused to let go. But in the stillness, I heard it clearly:

It's time. Time to stop surviving. Time to start living again.

"Sometimes the hardest part isn't letting go but learning to start over."

—Nicole Sobon

CHAPTER
Eight

PLANNING
THE LEAP

Once the decision to leave had taken root, the journey shifted from emotional turmoil to deliberate action.

Leaving a six-figure corporate job after more than 20 years wasn't just about handing in a resignation letter, it was about creating a roadmap for my future. One that balanced financial responsibility, personal healing, and the hope for something better.

I knew this wouldn't be a leap into the unknown. It would be a calculated jump, a carefully planned transition where every step mattered.

THE REALITY CHECK

The first thing I did was face the facts. I had a daughter heading off to college soon, there were tuition and expenses looming. That financial responsibility was a huge factor. I couldn't just walk away without a safety net. I had to be strategic. I needed to weigh every option, every risk, and every potential outcome.

BUILDING MY EXIT STRATEGY

I started by:

- Evaluating my finances: I took a hard look at savings, expenses, stocks, 401K options, and my family's budget.

- Exploring options: Could I freelance? Consult? Start a side hustle? What were my passions beyond the corporate world?

- Networking: Quietly reconnecting with trusted colleagues and mentors outside the company, discerning what opportunities might exist.

- Mental preparation: Recognizing the emotional pressure of leaving — the guilt, the uncertainty, the relief, and preparing myself to face it all.

SETTING BOUNDARIES

One of the hardest parts was learning to say no. Not just to others, but to the endless demands that had kept me tethered to a job that no longer served me.

I realized that before I could step fully into my new life, I had to protect my energy. That meant:

- Delegating more at work, even when it was uncomfortable.

- Taking time off to recharge: something I hadn't done in years.

- Prioritizing my family and my health.

- And most importantly, silencing the voice that told me I had to prove my worth through exhaustion.

THE FMLA BREAK

Eventually, I submitted a 30-day FMLA request — not to run away, but to make space. Space to breathe. To think. To be still long enough to hear myself again. And just as important, to be with my mother.

She was facing serious health concerns, and I knew I needed to be by her side. The timing was no coincidence. As everything in me was unraveling, being with her helped bring things back into focus. Family. Faith. What really mattered.

When my manager asked if I was okay, I told the truth. I shared that the emotional cost was becoming too high. It was one of the few moments I let the mask slip.

I didn't take the full 30 days of FMLA—the leave meant to protect employees when life overwhelms work. FMLA is there for situations where you need guaranteed time off, without the risk of losing your job. PTO, on the other hand, is the paid time off you accrue, often flexible but not protected in the same way.

Somehow, I let myself be talked out of the full FMLA. Instead, I took just a week of PTO. At the time, it felt like a compromise, a smaller, safer option—but it also came with a twinge of guilt and doubt. Did I let fear, pride, or the expectations of others guide my choice? Absolutely. It was stressful to say no to the FMLA, to shorten my leave, to convince myself this "smaller" plan was enough.

That brief week of PTO was only a hint of what I truly needed. It gave me a moment to breathe, to step back, and to face the reality I'd been avoiding: that my body, my mind, and my spirit were all signaling I couldn't keep going the way I had been.

Not long after returning, though, I realized I couldn't ignore the signals anymore. My body was sending clear warnings: fatigue, tension, the kind of burden that builds until it can no longer be pushed aside. I knew it was tied to the job, but even more to the challenges of working under my manager. This time, I followed through and submitted the request for FMLA.

What I didn't know then was just how critical that decision would become. That first official day away from work would lead me to an emergency doctor's appointment. I scheduled it with my PCP to understand what my body was trying to tell me.

Looking back, submitting that request wasn't just wise. It saved me in ways I couldn't have imagined... a choice that, if avoided, might have cost me everything.

THE SUPPORT SYSTEM

Throughout this process, I leaned heavily on my best friend, my family, and my daughter. Their encouragement grounded me.

I also prayed — seeking guidance, strength, and peace. God was and will always be my refuge. The one source that gave me the courage to take this leap of faith into the unknown.

It was my family and my friend's collective belief in me, and my faith, that became my anchor.

In those quiet moments away from the chaos, I began to see a new version of myself; one not defined by a job title or paycheck, but by purpose, passion, and peace.

I began sketching ideas, writing down dreams, and imagining a life where I was in control.

This chapter of planning wasn't just about logistics; it was about reclaiming my power.

"You don't have to have it all figured out to move forward."

— Unknown

CHAPTER
Nine

THE DAY EVERYTHING CHANGED

The day my FMLA officially began, I woke up telling my-self it would be just another day. No emails. No meet-ings. Just a doctor's appointment at 1:30 to finally figure out what my body had been trying to tell me. I didn't expect much—maybe a conversation, maybe some blood work. Nothing more.

But deep down, I think I already knew something was coming. You don't schedule that kind of appointment unless you sense a truth you've been avoiding.

I checked in at the front desk, sat in the waiting room scrolling through my phone, and then heard the nurse call my name. She walked me back, took my weight, then led me into an empty exam room and asked a few routine questions. When she reached for the blood pressure cuff, everything felt normal—just another appointment I'd been through dozens of times.

But when the cuff inflated on my left arm, I saw her face change. She let out a small breath as if she was trying not to alarm me, but her eyes betrayed her.

"Let me check your right arm," she said quietly.

I could hear the concern in her voice.

When she released the pressure and read the second number, her eyes told me everything before her words did. "Your blood pressure is very high," she said.

My stomach dropped.

That was the moment everything changed. My body was telling the truth my mind had been trying to ignore. Lately, the demands at work had pushed me to my breaking point, and I kept telling myself that if I just worked harder, stayed stronger, and kept going, I'd be fine. But sitting there, with tears in my eyes, I couldn't deny it any longer: the burden of stress wasn't just overwhelming, it was breaking me from the inside out.

THE MOMENT OF TRUTH

Up until then, I thought I had been handling things. Sure, the job was stressful. Sure, the meetings left me drained. Sure, I was constantly trying to prove myself while being pushed harder and harder. But I told myself, *That's just corporate life. That's just what it takes.*

I had ignored the headaches. I had ignored the sleepless nights. I had ignored the way my chest felt tight every Sunday night before the work week started.

But you can't ignore numbers. The blood pressure monitor doesn't lie.

It was as if God Himself was holding up a mirror and saying, *Do you see what this is doing to you? Do you see what you've allowed to happen?*

That day, sitting in the doctor's office, I knew something had to change. I couldn't just push through this anymore. I couldn't "work harder" or "tough it out." This wasn't about my pride or my performance. This was about my life.

My primary care physician came in shortly after the nurse left and talked to me about blood pressure medication, telling me we'd schedule a follow-up in two weeks. I nodded, but my mind was already spinning. I knew deep down… I could never go back to corporate America. Not after this.

THE QUIET RIDE HOME

On the drive home with my daughter in the passenger seat, it started to sink in. I told her my blood pressure was dangerously high and how grateful I was for the time off. I kept thinking how different things could have been if I hadn't made that appointment, I wouldn't have realized how close I'd been to the edge.

We didn't talk much. The ride was quiet, not because there was nothing to say, but because there was too much to say.

Silence has a way of saying what words can't. And in that silence, I made a decision I couldn't unmake.

For the first time in my life, I knew I had to choose me.

Not the company. Not the paycheck. Not the image of success I had worked so hard to build.

ME. MY HEALTH. MY LIFE.

Because here's the truth: you can always be replaced at a job. You can always be forgotten in a meeting. But your family can't replace you. Your life can't be replaced.

HOW STRESS SNEAKS UP ON US

That day was my breaking point, but maybe you've felt the warning signs too. Stress is sneaky. It doesn't show up overnight. It builds slowly, layer by layer, until one day you realize you're carrying more than your body or heart was ever designed to handle.

You brush off tension headaches. You laugh about being "too busy to sleep." You think it's normal to feel your stomach tied in knots every morning before work. But here's what I learned the hard way: **it's not normal**.

And the longer you ignore it, the louder your body will shout.

High blood pressure. Panic attacks. Burnout so deep you can't drag yourself out of bed.

I thought I was strong for pushing through. But strength isn't ignoring the warning signs. Strength is having the courage to stop and say, *I can't live like this anymore.*

GOD'S WAKE-UP CALL

Looking back, I believe that doctor's appointment was a divine interruption. It was God stepping into my story and saying, *Enough. You've given enough. You've endured enough. Now it's time to choose life.*

Sometimes God whispers through gentle nudges. Other times, He has to shake us awake. That day was my shaking.

The Bible says in John 10:10 that the enemy comes to steal, kill, and destroy—but Jesus came to give life, and life more abundantly.

What I was living wasn't abundant life. It was survival. Barely making it. Pushing through at the cost of my health, my joy, and my peace.

God wasn't calling me to keep sacrificing myself on the altar of a career. He was calling me back to life.

CORPORATE VS. CALLING

The reality is, corporate America doesn't care about your blood pressure. It doesn't care about your sleepless nights. As long as you show up, perform, and deliver results, you're valuable. The second you can't, you're replaceable.

That's the hard truth I had to face.

But God's calling is different. He cares about your heart. He cares about your health. He cares about whether you're living fully or just existing.

That day, I finally understood: no paycheck was worth my peace. No title was worth my health. No position was worth my life.

REFLECTION FOR YOU

Maybe you're reading this and feeling that same quiet tug inside yourself. Maybe your body is trying to tell you something. Maybe your mind has been screaming *slow down* and you've ignored it because it's inconvenient, or because you're afraid.

Ask yourself:

- Where am I ignoring the warning signs my body and soul are sending me?

- What am I sacrificing for success, titles, or appearances?

- If fear wasn't holding me back, what choice would I make today?

It's okay to stop. It's okay to say no. It's okay to step away from anything slowly eroding your peace, health, or joy.

PRACTICAL STEPS

1. **Listen to your body:** Notice tension, headaches, insomnia, or stress that feels constant. Don't dismiss it.

2. **Take a pause:** Even a small step back from responsibilities, meetings, or obligations can give your mind and body space to breathe.

3. **Reflect:** Ask yourself where you're sacrificing life for work. Where you're running on autopilot instead of living intentionally.

4. **Pray or meditate:** Invite God in. Ask Him to show you what belongs in your life and what doesn't.

5. **Take one action:** Do one concrete thing this week to protect your health or peace—say no, ask for help, or step back.

THE DAY MY LIFE CHANGED

That day marked a line in the sand for me. I knew I could never go back to that office. I could never go back to the cycle that was crushing me.

It was the day my blood pressure scared me into finally listening. But more than that, it was the day God showed me what I had been blind to: this job wasn't just stressful… it was slowly destroying me.

And in His mercy, He gave me a way out.

I didn't just walk away from corporate America that day. I walked toward life. I walked toward healing. I walked toward the person God created me to be.

It was the day everything changed. And I believe He wants to give you that kind of day too.

CHAPTER
Ten

THE RESIGNATION

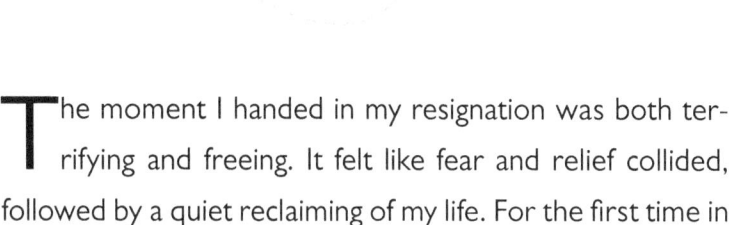

The moment I handed in my resignation was both terrifying and freeing. It felt like fear and relief collided, followed by a quiet reclaiming of my life. For the first time in a long time, I was choosing myself.

After two decades of giving everything to a system that didn't see or understand my worth, walking away wasn't easy. But staying? That would've cost me everything—my peace, my health, my joy.

THE CONVERSATION

I had rehearsed what I would say many times, but when the moment came, I kept it simple. I submitted my resignation calmly and professionally. No drama, no finger-pointing; just the truth. It was time to move on for my own growth, healing, and future. Though leaving the team I cared for was difficult, and I knew I would miss them deeply, I found peace in knowing I chose to leave with honesty and dignity.

THE AFTERMATH

What followed was a flood of emotions. Grief. Relief. Uncertainty. Excitement. I had traded a predictable path for the unknown, and it was both thrilling and terrifying.

My friends showed up for me. My team expressed their love and appreciation. It reminded me that even in broken systems, the impact we make on people is real.

EMBRACING THE UNKNOWN

Letting go of a six-figure salary wasn't just about income. It was about rewriting the script. I wasn't just stepping away from corporate life, I was stepping into who I was becoming.

I was no longer bound by job titles or office politics. I was becoming the entrepreneur of my own life. And though I didn't have all the answers, I had my freedom.

And that was enough to begin.

REFLECTION

Looking back, handing in that resignation wasn't the end. It was the turning point. A line in the sand. A declaration that I am not what I do. I am not my title. I am not what I earn.

I am worthy, period.

And walking away was the moment I started walking toward something real.

" *"And when you finally let go, you realize it's not the end, but the start of something new."*

—Unknown

CHAPTER
Eleven

NEW BEGINNINGS: WRITING MY OWN STORY

For over twenty years, corporate America was the stage of my life. A place where I climbed the ladder, earned promotions, and built teams. But underneath the meetings and the suits, another world lived quietly inside me—a world of words and stories waiting to be told.

Writing has always been my refuge. Even after the longest days, I gave what little time I had—after hours, late nights, and weekends—to write. It took discipline. It required sacrifice. But more than anything, it felt like answering a call I could no longer ignore. Over time, that quiet passion grew into something tangible—seven published books, articles in a respected Christian magazine, and over one hundred blogs on my website.

Each book holds a piece of my heart: a reflection of faith, struggle, and victory. The articles gave me a platform to share hope rooted in God's grace. But the blogs? They became a lifeline. A way to speak directly to people who were hurting, questioning, and searching—reminding them they weren't walking alone. God was with them. Every step of the way.

Yet for years, this part of me stayed in the shadows; a parallel life I nurtured but kept separate from my corporate identity.

My family and friends saw what I sometimes tried to hide from myself—the light that writing brought to my eyes, the way my face would brighten when talking about a new idea. They urged me again and again to stop waiting for the "right moment." Make writing your full-time pursuit.

One evening, a conversation with a trusted spiritual mentor stopped me in my tracks. The message was clear, so powerful that I put the phone on speaker for my daughter to hear.

"You've already built something incredible with your writing," she said. "Why wait any longer to let the world see it? You don't have to stay in a job that's draining you. You have the talent, the experience, and the heart to make this work."

My daughter nodded and said, "Dad, you inspire so many people with your words. It's time you did it for you."

Their words echoed in my mind long after the call ended. It wasn't just encouragement, it was a call to courage. To action.

Leaving a six-figure salary wasn't a light decision. With my daughter preparing for college, financial security mattered. That safety net was comforting, even if it cost my peace.

But with every day in that corporate world, pieces of myself slipped further away.

I realized writing and building this new venture weren't hobbies. They were lifelines.

With my family and friends' support, I started planning. I leaned into the skills I'd honed over years: branding, communication, leadership, and applied them to my own journey.

The process was both exciting and terrifying. Doubts whispered—Could I really do this? Would people accept me outside a corporate title? What if I failed?

But those fears were drowned out by a deeper freedom. For the first time in a long time, I was creating something that belonged solely to me, with nothing holding me back.

Writing became more than a career pivot, it became therapy, mission, and the way I reclaimed my voice. It healed wounds left by toxic leadership and restored my confidence.

Readers reached out, sharing how my words had touched their lives—the greatest validation I could hope for.

As I stepped into this new chapter, I've learned that freedom isn't the absence of fear. It's choosing to move forward anyway.

The story I'm writing now isn't just about leaving corporate America. It's about embracing purpose, passion, and peace—on my own terms.

And this is only the beginning.

CHAPTER

Twelve

WHO I AM NOW

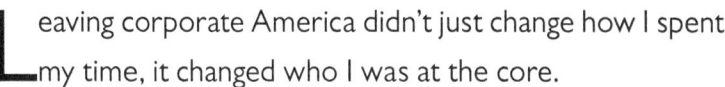

Leaving corporate America didn't just change how I spent my time, it changed who I was at the core.

It forced me to slow down and take inventory of who I had become, and more importantly, who I had always been beneath the pressure, the titles, and the performance. For so long, my identity had been wrapped up in what I did, what I accomplished, and how well I did it. I didn't realize how deeply the role had defined the man.

The truth is—I didn't know how much of myself I had buried under the pressure of trying to be "enough." Enough for the job. Enough for the expectations. Enough for everyone who depended on me.

There's something about always being the reliable one —the steady hand in chaos that makes it easy to lose sight of your own heart. You get so used to holding everyone else together that you don't notice you're quietly coming undone. I was so focused on being who others needed me to be that I stopped asking whether I was still being who God called me to be.

It didn't happen all at once. You don't wake up one day and say, "I'm lost." It's gradual. It's subtle. You feel it in the moments when your passion starts to fade. When the things that once energized you start to drain you. When you can't remember the last time you felt fully alive in the work you're doing.

But we keep going. We tell ourselves it's just a season. Just a tough quarter. Just a difficult boss. Just stress. Just burnout. Just life.

But eventually, you run out of excuses. And if you're being honest, you realize it's not just the job that's off, it's *you*.

That's where I found myself. Not broken, but tired. Not empty but poured out. Not angry, just…done.

And once I walked away, I had to face a truth that felt equal parts sobering and freeing. I had spent years building a version of myself that made sense on paper but didn't align with who I truly was anymore.

So who am I now—without the deadlines, the business cards, or the title attached to my name?

Honestly, I'm still discovering the full answer to that question; but for the first time in a long time, I'm asking it from a healthy place. I'm not asking it to find a new box to fit in. I'm not asking it so I can brand myself better or be more marketable. I'm asking it because I want to live from a place of alignment, spiritually, emotionally, and mentally.

That takes work. And not the kind of work that comes with a paycheck or performance review.

It's the work of soul-searching. The work of healing. The work of unlearning. The work of letting go of who I thought I had to be in order to become who I truly am.

And here's what I've discovered so far:

I am not my title.

I am not my salary.

I am not my LinkedIn bio or the letters after my name.

I'm a man of vision.

A man of integrity.

A man who leads with heart.

A man who chooses purpose over popularity.

A man who values peace more than performance.

Walking away helped me see the places where my worth had been unknowingly tethered to the wrong things. Because sometimes, the only way to see how something has shaped you—is to step away from it completely.

I thought I would miss the validation. I thought I would struggle with the silence. I thought I'd wake up every day second-guessing my decision.

But what surprised me most? I started breathing again—deeply, freely, without pressure chasing every inhale.

There was a peace that came with not having to prove anything. A freedom in knowing that I didn't have to keep climbing a ladder that God never told me to climb. A joy in realizing that the real me, the one who had dreams outside of boardrooms and meetings was still there, still alive, still capable of thriving.

I began reconnecting with the passions I had sidelined. Writing. Teaching. Building. Encouraging others. Pouring into the next generation. Creating things that last. These weren't just hobbies, they were pieces of my calling that had been buried under the demands of responsibility.

And slowly, I started to settle into a new routine. One not dictated by deadlines, but by discernment. One rooted in obedience, not optics. One that allows room for grace, rest, creativity, and real impact.

I'm not saying it's easy. There are still moments where doubt tries to creep in. Moments where I wonder if I made the right choice. Moments where I miss the predictability of a steady paycheck or the respect that came with a certain title.

But those moments are fleeting. They're not loud enough to drown out the truth I now carry: This was never just about leaving a job. It was about becoming whole.

It was about giving myself permission to live from a place of authenticity. To lead from the inside out. To be present, not just productive. To find peace without needing to earn it.

And maybe for the first time in my life, that's exactly what success looks like.

This is who I am now: A man who listens when God speaks. A man who values obedience over how things look. A man who shows up, fully, freely, and without apology. A man who believes that freedom is worth the risk. A man who no longer fears quiet seasons, because he knows God does His best work in them.

My story didn't end when I left the job. It actually began.

And I'm learning that when your identity is rooted in God…not in what you do or what others think, you don't have to be afraid of change. You don't have to fear starting over. You don't even have to have it all figured out.

You just have to stay grounded in truth.

So, if you're reading this and you're wondering who you are now that everything has changed—whether you walked away, got pushed out, or are just in a season of transition, let me encourage you—you're not lost. You're just being reintroduced to yourself.

And the version of you on the other side of this? You're stronger. Wiser. Clearer. Freer. And more aligned with who God always knew you were.

Let the world keep its boxes. Let others chase titles and trophies. You've been called to something deeper. Something more honest. More meaningful. More eternal.

Who you are now isn't someone who failed. You're someone who had the **courage to change.**

CHAPTER

Thirteen

REDEFINING SUCCESS

There was a time when success was easy to define. It looked like a title with real meaning behind it. A salary that made people pause. A résumé full of recognizable names and impressive achievements. It was the corner office, the steady climb up the ladder, the perks, and the "you made it" nods from people who had no idea how much it was costing me to keep it all together.

For a while, I wore that version of success like armor. It shielded me from questions I wasn't ready to face—questions about purpose, peace, and fulfillment. I convinced myself that as long as I was producing and providing, I was winning. That was the goal. That was enough.

But what happens when the life you built starts to feel more like a cage than a reward?

What happens when you check every box and still feel empty?

That question stayed with me. Because success isn't just about what we achieve, it's also about what we're afraid to lose. For me, success had become a kind of survival. It made me feel safe, seen, and validated. But deep down, I knew I was being called to redefine it.

Not tweak it. Not find a new balance. Redefine it entirely.

LETTING GO OF EXTERNAL VALIDATION

The first step was confronting how much I had come to rely on external affirmation. I didn't realize how deeply I had tied my worth to how others perceived me. When people praised my work ethic, I took it as confirmation that I mattered. When they applauded my leadership, I felt useful. Seen.

But if you're going to redefine success, you have to separate affirmation from identity. You have to ask yourself: *If no one applauds, would I still feel like I'm enough?*

That question hit me hard.

Because I saw how often I had been performing instead of living. Serving instead of being. Grinding instead of growing. Hoping that someone would say, "You're doing great."

But I don't need the world to tell me I'm doing well if I know I'm walking in obedience.

I had to learn how to live for an audience of One. Not in a surface-level way, but in a quiet, life-altering way. I started asking God -- *Am I in alignment with You?*

When I let go of chasing approval, something shifted. I stopped needing validation and started valuing vision.

WHAT SUCCESS LOOKS LIKE NOW

Today, success looks different.

It looks like peace in the morning. It looks like choosing how I spend my time, who I pour into, and what deserves my energy. It means protecting my boundaries, guarding my spirit, and refusing to trade my well-being for a paycheck or applause.

Success means saying no when something doesn't sit right in my spirit, even if it's lucrative or looks good on paper. It means choosing purpose over popularity, truth over appearances.

It's not glamorous. The income isn't guaranteed. The answers aren't always clear. But freedom is real. And the joy? It's deep, steady, and unshakable.

I don't measure success by how high I climb, but by how aligned I am—both outwardly and inwardly. Not by how many people follow me, but by how faithfully I follow God.

Ironically, the moment I stopped chasing what the world calls success, I started experiencing everything I thought success would bring: peace, clarity, fulfillment, and purpose.

RETHINKING SUCCESS

This isn't just my story. It's for anyone who's stuck in a version of success that no longer fits.

Especially professionals—men and women who fought hard to build something only to realize it doesn't feel like home anymore. We live in a culture that idolizes hustle, rewards burnout, and glorifies the grind.

But we were never meant to live that way.

We're more than what we do. More than what we produce. More than any title or role we hold.

So, what if we gave ourselves permission to redefine success?

What if success wasn't about achievement, but alignment? What if we stopped asking, "What do you do?" and started asking, "How's your soul?" What if the most radical, courageous thing we could do was protect our peace and tell the truth about what we really need?

For men and women in corporate America especially, the pressure is relentless. Be strong but not intimidating.

Be kind but not soft. Be excellent but not too ambitious. The expectations are endless, and the rewards are often shallow.

It's no wonder so many of us are exhausted.

But this book isn't about walking away from work. *It's about waking up to who you really are.*

Because staying in something that costs you your peace, your voice, or your identity isn't noble. It's *self-neglect*.

You don't have to keep proving your worth to people who wouldn't even notice if you disappeared.

You don't have to stay in rooms where your calling is being minimized just because the salary is maximized.

The truth is—you can be praised and still be out of alignment. You can be promoted and still feel empty. You can be respected and still feel completely disconnected from purpose.

That's not success. That's survival in a suit.

EMBRACING YOUR OWN SUCCESS

Real success looks like peace in the middle of pressure. It's living in alignment with your values and purpose, wherever you find yourself.

It's setting healthy boundaries, saying no when you need to, and taking time to rest and recharge.

It's hearing a quiet assurance inside that you are enough, not because of what you do, but because of who you are.

When your peace is steady, your identity secure, and your purpose clear—that is success worth pursuing.

It's less about doing more and more but about becoming the person you were always meant to be.

No matter your job or season, you can embrace this kind of success.

And that is something truly worth holding onto.

CHAPTER
Fourteen

FOR ANYONE WHO'S THINKING ABOUT LEAVING

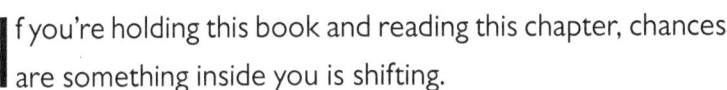

If you're holding this book and reading this chapter, chances are something inside you is shifting.

Maybe it started as a quiet discomfort. A subtle nudge that the space you're in—the role, the rhythm, the environment—no longer fits who you're becoming. Maybe you've asked yourself, "Can I really keep doing this?"

You might be brushing those thoughts aside. Or you've spiritualized them away, convincing yourself that discomfort means disobedience. Or maybe, in the stillness of your alone time, you've been crying silent tears, exhausted from holding on to something that no longer feels true to who you are.

I've been there. And before we go any further, let me make something clear:

You are not crazy. You are not weak. You are not being dramatic. *You are waking up.*

You're beginning to discern the difference between *what looks good* and *what actually is good* for you. And that awareness? *It's a gift.*

Leaving something stable—especially something you worked hard for—isn't something people do lightly. I'm not here to hand you a formula or tell you what your next move should be. But I am here to tell the truth.

Because I know what it's like to sit in a position that checks all the boxes on paper: status, salary, success, but feels like a slow erosion of who you really are.

You don't have to reach a breaking point before you choose peace. You don't need permission to listen to the whisper of God pulling you in a new direction.

If you've been thinking about leaving, really thinking about it, here are some things to consider:

1. Feeling Undervalued Isn't Ingratitude: It's a Signal

Some people will try to guilt you into staying. They'll say you should be grateful. That it's not *that* bad. That other people have it worse.

But here's the truth: being undervalued is not a character-building exercise from God. It's a signal that something is off.

You can be thankful for what a place gave you and still be honest about what it's taking from you.

God did not call you to be a doormat for the sake of being "nice." He did not gift you with discernment only to have you ignore it for the sake of being agreeable. If the environment you're in is draining your spirit, it may be time to ask God: *Am I still called here?*

And if the answer is no, obedience matters more than approval.

2. The Exit Doesn't Have to Be Perfect: Just Honest

Let go of the idea that leaving has to look polished. That you need a five-year plan, a backup salary, and a public announcement.

Sometimes, all you get is a deep knowing. A quiet conviction that says, *It's time.*

Leaving doesn't mean you have no plan, but don't let perfectionism keep you stuck. Faith often requires motion before clarity. I didn't leave with all the details locked in. I left with peace in my spirit and the voice of God saying, "Go."

Planning is wise. Obedience is essential. Waiting for perfect timing? That might just be fear in disguise.

3. Start Preparing, Even If You're Not Leaving Tomorrow

You don't have to leave next week. But if you feel the shift, start moving in alignment now.

Ask yourself: What have I lost in this space that I need to reclaim?

What am I tolerating that I wouldn't advise someone I love to accept?

What kind of life do I truly want, and what does God say about it?

Start planting seeds. Maybe that's setting a boundary. Or reviving a passion. Or reconnecting with people who remind you of who you are. This is preparation. And preparation is an act of faith.

4. Learn to Trust Yourself Again

Toxic systems train you to doubt your voice. You start apologizing for your boundaries. You second-guess your instincts. You wonder if it's all in your head.

But it's not.

God gave you that voice. That discernment. That feeling in your gut that says, *This isn't it.*

You're not broken. You were in a space that made you feel like your strength was a liability. That's not truth. That's control.

This next season? It requires you to trust what God is showing you, even if others don't see it yet.

5. Leaving Isn't Quitting, It's Obedience

People will call it quitting. Some will call it reckless. Others might see it as failure.

Let them talk.

They didn't hear what God whispered to you at 2 a.m. They don't know how long you've been praying for clarity. They can't feel the ache in your chest when Sunday night rolls around.

God does.

And He's not asking you to convince others. He's asking you to follow Him. Leaving isn't weakness. It takes strength to walk away from something everyone else claps for.

You're not running. You're choosing alignment.

6.   You Are Not Alone

This part might feel isolating. People don't always understand when you step away from security.

But I promise you, you are not the only one God is calling into more.

There are others walking this road. Others who chose faith over fear. Others who rebuilt from the rubble. And every one of us has the scars to prove it.

But we also have joy. Peace. Purpose. And freedom.

You're not leaving your calling behind. You're reclaiming it. You're not abandoning your purpose. You're rediscovering it. You're not giving up.

You're rising up.

SOME PRACTICAL NEXT STEPS

1. Pray for clarity and courage. Ask God for both direction and the boldness to follow it.

2. Create a simple exit plan. Outline your financial needs, list your non-negotiables, and sketch a short-term strategy.

3. Write down your vision. Even if it's blurry, start writing what stirs in your spirit.

4. Find safe, wise counsel. Talk with people who won't just affirm your fears but will call out your faith.

5. Revisit your "why." Journal. Reflect. Let God remind you of the conviction that led you here.

You don't need all the answers. You just need enough faith for the next step.

Leaving isn't failure. It's faith.

And faith, when followed, always leads to freedom.

So if you've been thinking about leaving—maybe it's because God is already leading you.

CHAPTER

Fifteen

PEACE OVER PAYCHECKS

There comes a moment in every journey of faith when you realize that what you walked away from is no match for what you've gained.

For me, that moment didn't arrive with a big announcement. It didn't show up on the day I turned in my resignation. It didn't come with the launch of something new. It came in the quiet….when I realized I no longer carried the anxiety that used to show up like clockwork every Sunday night. When I woke up and didn't feel dread or heaviness before the day even began. When I could hear God clearly, not because He hadn't been speaking, but because *I was finally still enough to listen.*

That's when I knew: I didn't just leave a job. I found peace.

Real peace. Not the temporary kind that comes with a weekend off or a canceled meeting. Not the "finally caught up on emails" peace. But the kind that guards your heart and mind even when the income isn't steady and the path isn't clear. It turns out—peace was the paycheck I was always chasing.

CHOOSING YOURSELF AGAIN AND AGAIN

When people hear that I left a six-figure salary to follow a quieter, purpose-filled path, they often respond with admiration, or concern. "That's brave," they say. Or "I could never do that." Some ask, "But what do you do now?" Others just pause, unsure of what to make of it.

But here's what I've learned: You don't have to explain peace to people who've never lived without it.

Most people are just trying to survive. We've been conditioned to believe that the higher the salary, the higher our value. That if the numbers look right, life must be good. That if we're climbing, it must be worth it. But here's the hard truth I had to face: *if you're constantly trading your peace for a paycheck, the cost is too high.*

I had to choose myself again...not from ego, but from obedience. I had to choose my health. My creativity. My rest. My calling. My family. My joy. And not just once, but over and over again.

Because even after you leave, the temptation to go back is real. There will be days when fear whispers, "You made a mistake." Days when comparison clouds your clarity. Days when lack tries to convince you that it was better back there. That's when you remember the *why*. That's when you go back to the promise. *Peace* was never the easy choice, but *it was always the right one*.

LOSS OR LIBERATION?

To some, walking away looks like a loss. A loss of stability. A loss of status. A loss of all you worked so hard to build. And I get it: by the world's definition, it might be.

But I didn't experience it as a loss. I experienced it as liberation.

I gained my time back. My joy. My clarity. I created space for what mattered most. I gained freedom to say yes to God's assignments without forcing them into the cracks of someone else's agenda. I gained myself back.

And even now, with all the unknowns, I wouldn't trade this for anything. Because no amount of income is worth sacrificing your well-being. No promotion can replace peace. No title can compete with alignment.

Peace is the kind of wealth that doesn't fluctuate with the market. And if you could put a price on it, it would still be worth more than anything you'd earn chasing someone else's version of success.

NOT EVERYONE WILL UNDERSTAND: AND THAT'S OKAY

When you choose peace, not everyone will get it.

Some will question your decisions. Some will distance themselves. Others might project their fears onto your faith. And you know what? That's okay.

You're not here to make sense to everyone. You're here to be obedient to God.

The more I walk this path, the more I see how much people crave permission. They watch from the sidelines and think, *I want that too.* Not the job title. Not the platform. The peace. The freedom. The joy.

And that's why your story matters. Because it shows what's possible. You become living proof that faith is not just a belief, it's a way of life. You show people what it looks like to move before it all makes sense. To trust God over comfort. To say yes, even when it costs you.

You don't have to be fearless. You just have to be faithful.

PROVISION STILL COMES

Let me be clear: this road hasn't been without its valleys.

There were months I had to believe God for every single dollar. Moments when I questioned if I'd misheard Him. Nights when I stared at the ceiling and wondered how it would all work out. But every single time, provision came.

Not always how I expected. Not always when I wanted. But always.

God opened doors I didn't know existed. He brought opportunities through unexpected connections. He sent reminders, through people and moments, that I was never walking alone.

Provision may look different now. But it's more than enough. Because God funds what He favors. He sustains what He calls. He shows up for what He authors. Every. Single. Time.

You're Not Just Walking Away. You're Walking Into.

This journey isn't about abandoning responsibility or chasing a feel-good moment. It's about alignment. Obedience. Faith.

You're not just walking away from a job, a title, or a paycheck. You're walking into purpose. Into clarity. Into communion with God.

You're walking into a version of your life where you no longer have to fake contentment. Where you can breathe deeply, live fully, and serve freely.

You're walking into who God always created you to be.

And that? That's the kind of success no one can take from you.

FINAL REFLECTIONS

So, as we close this chapter, and this book…I want to leave you with this:

You are allowed to want more than survival. You are allowed to choose peace. You are allowed to walk away. You are allowed to start again. You are allowed to live a life that feels like your own.

You don't need anyone's permission to change. God already gave it to you when He started stirring your heart.

He's already gone ahead of you. He's already made the way. Now it's your turn to follow.

You're not crazy. You're being called. You're not irresponsible. You're being released. You're not abandoning your purpose. You're walking straight into it.

Peace is waiting.

Not after the next title.

Not after the next raise.

Not once everything is figured out.

Peace is on the other side of obedience.

So choose it. And don't look back.

Oh, and one last thing… They thought I walked away empty-handed. But what they couldn't see was that obedience unlocked a purpose-driven life. One that now produces peace, impact, and income beyond anything I left behind.

The Journey Ahead

I f you made it to this page, I want to say something simple and true: You're not alone.

You're not the only one who's questioned your worth, struggled with your calling, or walked away from something that once defined you. You're not the only one who's had to relearn how to breathe, how to trust God again, how to believe that peace was even possible.

But here you are. And whether you're still in the middle of your decision or already living it out: this is *holy* ground. God has not wasted a single chapter of your story. Not the hard ones. Not the hidden ones. Not the ones you thought would break you. He's been with you through every high and every valley, shaping you for the very thing you're walking into now.

This is not the end of your story. This is just the beginning of one that you and God will write together.

So don't rush it. Don't fear it. And don't apologize for it.

There's purpose in your pause. Glory in your obedience. And power in your peace.

The world doesn't need more people performing. It needs more people surrendered. And your surrender just might be the miracle someone else is waiting to see.

So take the next step. And then the next. Let grace lead. Let God provide. And let peace be your confirmation.

You don't have to prove anything. *You just have to follow.*

Closing Prayer

Father God,

Thank You for never leaving me, even in the places I stayed too long, and even in the moments I didn't know how to let go. Thank You for being patient with me while I struggled with fear, with identity, with disappointment, and with doubt. You saw the burden I carried. You heard the prayers I didn't have words for. You met me in the breaking, and You've been faithful in the rebuilding. God, I give You what's left of my fear and I take hold of what You've promised: peace, purpose, and freedom. Help me walk boldly into the life You've called me to live. Not the life that looks good on paper, but the one that breathes life into my soul. Teach me how to move forward with grace, with wisdom, and with courage. Let Your voice be louder than fear. Let Your presence be stronger than the pressure. Let Your peace go before me in every decision I make. Remind me that I'm not too late. That I'm not too far behind. That I haven't missed it.

Because You are the Author of my story, and You're still writing. So I surrender the pen again today. Lead me, Lord. And I will follow.

In Jesus' name, Amen.